W9-BKI-631

KILLER ANIMALS

COBRAS

ON THE HUNT

by Janet Riehecky

Reading Consultant:
Barbara J. Fox
Reading Specialist
North Carolina State University

Content Consultants:
Joe Maierhauser, President/CEO
Terry Phillip, Curator of Reptiles
Reptile Gardens
Rapid City, South Dakota

Capstone
press

Mankato, Minnesota

Blazers is published by Capstone Press,
151 Good Counsel Drive, P.O. Box 669, Mankato, Minnesota 56002.
www.capstonepress.com

Library of Congress Cataloging-in-Publication Data
Riehecky, Janet, 1953–
    Cobras: on the hunt/by Janet Riehecky.
    p. cm. — (Blazers. Killer animals.)
    Includes bibliographical references and index.
    Summary: "Describes cobras, their physical features, how they hunt and kill, and their role in the ecosystem" — Provided by publisher.
    ISBN-13: 978-1-4296-2317-9 (hardcover)
    ISBN-10: 1-4296-2317-9 (hardcover)
    1. Cobras — Juvenile literature. I. Title.
QL666.O64R54 2009
597.96'42 — dc22   2008029840

Editorial Credits
Abby Czeskleba, editor; Kyle Grenz, designer; Wanda Winch, photo researcher

Photo Credits
Bruce Coleman Inc./Lynn M. Stone, 24; Norman Myers, 18–19
Getty Images Inc./AFP/Michael Mathes, 26–27; National Geographic/Mattias Klum, 6
José Bergada Photography, photographersdirect.com, 9
Kimballstock.com/Ron Kimball, cover
Nature Picture Library/Mary McDonald, 20–21; Michael Richards/John Downer, 10–11;
    Tony Phelps, 15
Paul Brehem Film & Photography, photographersdirect.com, 28–29
Peter Arnold/Biosphoto/Marcon Brigitte, 22–23; WILDLIFE, 5
Rodney Byfield, photographersdirect.com, 12–13
Will Moody Photography, photographersdirect.com, 17

1 2 3 4 5 6 14 13 12 11 10 09

TABLE OF CONTENTS

SNAKE STRIKE

A cobra quietly **slithers** through the grass. Its tongue darts in and out of its mouth. It smells another snake nearby. The cobra slowly lifts its head above the grass.

slither – to slide across the ground by twisting back and forth

4

The cobra sees the snake. Suddenly, the cobra springs forward and sinks its **fangs** into the snake. The snake cannot move. The cobra swallows it whole.

fang – a long, pointed tooth

WEAPONS OF A KILLER

Cobras are fierce **reptiles**. Most are 3 to 10 feet (.9 to 3 meters) long. King cobras can grow up to 18 feet (5.5 meters) long. Most cobras weigh less than 6 pounds (2.7 kilograms).

reptile – a scaly-skinned animal that has the same body temperature as its surroundings

Cobras have sharp, hollow fangs. **Venom** flows through the fangs. Venom goes into an animal's body when the cobra bites it.

venom – a poisonous liquid produced by some snakes

KILLER FACT

Some cobras can spray venom up
to 8 feet (2.4 meters).

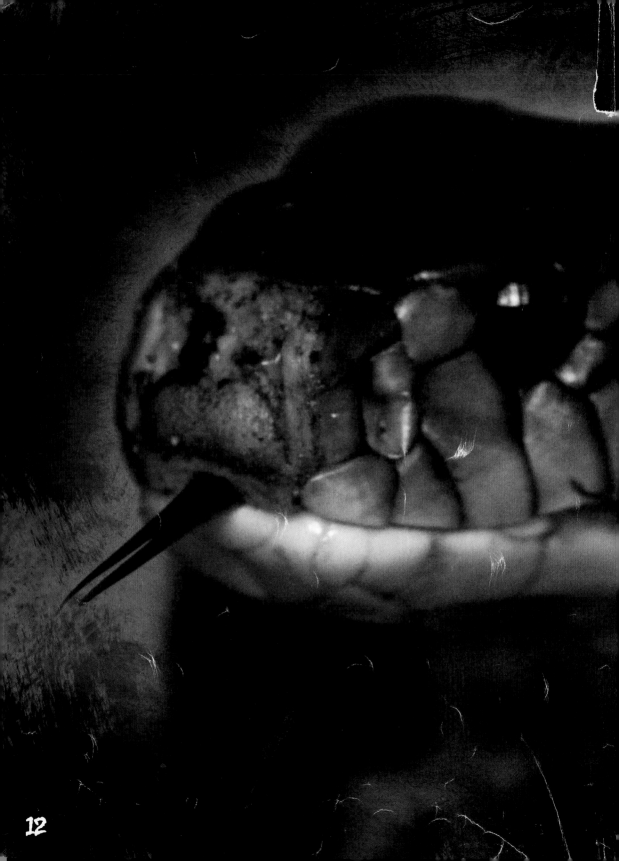

Most cobras cannot see animals from far away. They also cannot hear noises in the air. Cobras sense sounds through the ground. They know **prey** is nearby when the ground moves.

prey – an animal hunted by another animal

Cobras also hunt prey using their strong sense of smell. A cobra's tongue picks up scents and carries them to the **Jacobson's organ**. The Jacobson's organ can lead a snake to its next meal.

Jacobson's organ – an organ on the roof of the mouth of a reptile

HUNTING FOR FOOD

Cobras hunt alone. They look for lizards, small animals, and other snakes to eat.

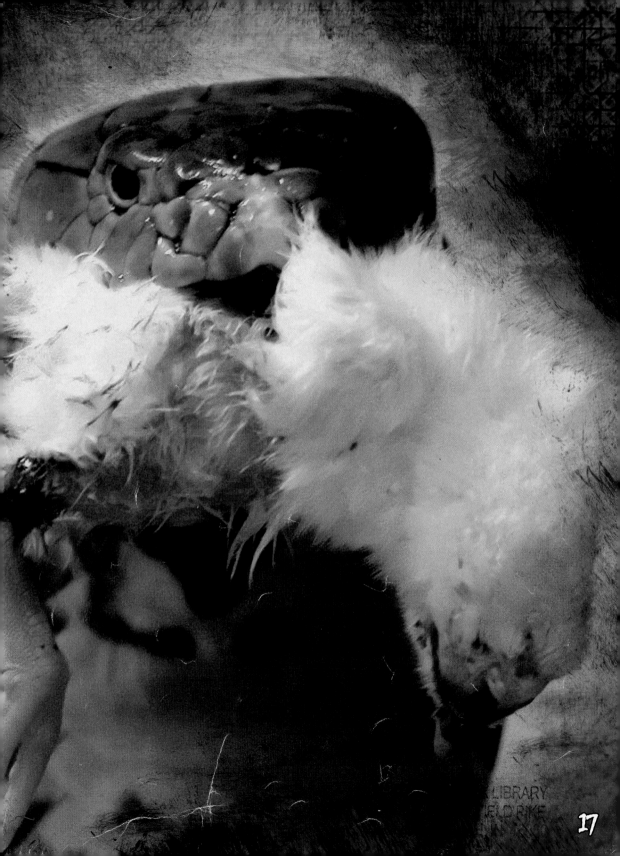

17

hood – part of a cobra's neck; a cobra creates its hood by sticking out its ribs.

If an animal scares a cobra, the snake will raise part of its body off the ground. The snake may also spread its **hood**. The cobra then charges forward and tries to bite the animal.

The snake's venom **paralyzes** prey. The animal cannot move or breathe. Then the cobra swallows it whole.

paralyze – to cause a loss of the ability to control the muscles

KILLER FACT

The jaws of a cobra can stretch apart. The snake can eat prey wider than its head.

Cobra Diagram

skinny tail

scaly skin

forked tongue

hood

HELPING THE ECOSYSTEM

Cobras play an important role in the **ecosystem**. They eat birds, lizards, snakes, and other animals. Without cobras, there would be too many animals of one kind. Too many animals can be bad for the ecosystem.

ecosystem – a group of animals and plants that work together with their surroundings

Most people are afraid of cobras. But cobras do not usually attack humans unless they feel scared. People must respect these dangerous snakes.

On the Attack!

29

GLOSSARY

ecosystem (EE-koh-sis-tuhm) — a group of animals and plants that work together with their surroundings

fang (FANG) — a long, pointed tooth

hood (HOOD) — part of a cobra's neck; a cobra creates its hood by sticking out its ribs.

Jacobson's organ (JAY-kuhb-suhnz OR-guhn) — an organ on the roof of a reptile's mouth

paralyze (PA-ruh-lize) — to cause a loss of the ability to control the muscles

prey (PRAY) — an animal hunted by another animal for food

reptile (REP-tile) — a scaly-skinned animal that has the same body temperature as its surroundings

slither (SLITH-ur) — to slide across the ground by twisting back and forth

venom (VEN-uhm) — a poisonous liquid produced by some snakes

READ MORE

Bredeson, Carmen. *Fun Facts About Snakes!* I Like Reptiles and Amphibians! Berkeley Heights, N.J.: Enslow, 2008.

Johnson, Sylvia A. *Cobras.* Nature Watch. Minneapolis: Lerner, 2007.

Landau, Elaine. *Big Snakes: Hunters of the Night.* Animals After Dark. Berkeley Heights, N.J.: Enslow, 2008.

INTERNET SITES

FactHound offers a safe, fun way to find educator-approved Internet sites related to this book.

Here's what you do:

1. Visit *www.facthound.com*
2. Choose your grade level.
3. Begin your search.

This book's ID number is 9781429623179.

FactHound will fetch the best sites for you!

INDEX